Living The

Mango-Licious Life

SIPS & TIPS ON SURVIVING AND THRIVING BEYOND SEASONS OF ADVERSITY

#Cancerwarrior #preemiemom #overcomer

TANYA WILSON

Printed in the United States of America

ISBN: 978-1-7357616-2-6

Kingdomboss Publishing

MEET THE AUTHOR:

Tanya Wilson was born in Kingston, Jamaica.

She obtained a bachelor's degree in economics from Florida Atlantic University. After graduating with her master's degree in urban planning from the University of Maryland, Tanya has spent the last twenty years working as an urban planner both domestically in the United States as well as internationally with her work in China. Tanya has left an impression on many significant community development initiatives throughout South Florida. She has earned numerous awards in her current position as a planning director with a local government agency.

Tanya enjoys participating in community service projects with her church's youth group. One of her greatest hobbies is discovering and sampling new varieties of mangoes. Tanya shares inspirational experiences in her blog, *Tanya, the Mango Lady*, which has been featured on National Public Radio.

Her proudest achievement to date has been serving as mother to two witty, rambunctious, and endlessly curious girls, Jada and Moriah.

Preface

The mango-licious life can be characterized by its resilience--a fierce resolve to live with fullness and purpose despite life's servings of sweet and sour seasons. This book is inspired by my journey. Throughout my life, I have encountered many adversities including childhood trauma, complications during childbirth, a life-threatening terminal illness, and strained familial relationships. However, with each bitter tragedy, God has taught me to persevere. I sip my cup of mango-aide and savor the sweetness this life still has to offer.

The title of this book also pays homage to the mango, my favorite fruit. The mango serves as a parody for life's unpredictable and often bittersweet journey. Yet in so many cultures the mango epitomizes all that is sweet, satisfying, and savory. I hope this book provides a window of inspiration, insight, and sustenance for others. I trust you will gain strength and empowerment from my stories as you heal, overcome and grow despite your difficult season(s).

I want you to know there is still room in your life for abundance, joy, and fulfillment beyond your tragedies. The mango-licious life is a mindset shared by those who not only survive but thrive beyond life's most difficult seasons. As we travel through each story, I hope you will find purpose, flavor, and renewed hope for the road ahead.

Join me now on an insightful journey as we explore metaphorical mango seasons, stop, sip, and reflect on lessons learned. Through each chapter, we will travel from bitter to sweet, and from lighthearted to deep. Be inspired to press on in hope and freedom as you too, embrace that mango-licious life.

Acknowledgements:

I am thankful for my village of friends, family, and colleagues. You nudged, seed planted, and encouraged me to write this book. You are part of my mango-licious life.

To my two incredible daughters Moriah and Jada, you are both the sun in my shine and the wave that propels me forward. I thank God for you daily and pray you both gain strength and inspiration from my life stories.

To my Lord and Savior Jesus Christ, I have come this far only by faith and your grace. It's within you that I live, move, and have my being. Grateful, thankful, blessed.

Table of Contents:

Chapter 1One

Love Affair: The Juicy Details

"There is a time for everything, and a season for every activity under the heavens"
Ecclesiastes 3:1

The month of June is celebrated in the United States as National Mango Month. Truthfully, mango lovers can't be restrained to just one month of celebrating this golden symbol of sweetness and sheer goodness. Celebrations for the "King of Fruits" are dropping all year long, across the Caribbean, Latin America, Africa, and Asia. Adoring mango fans love these celebrations. And why not? Fibrous or smooth, oblong or oval, mangoes are the ultimate comfort food.

Mangoes outrival all other fruits in flavor, color, and nostalgic appeal. This majestic fruit even has its own day! In the United States of America, July 22 is National Mango Day (ok, don't judge me for knowing that!). The mango is the great equalizer that transcends color, class, and creed and reigns supreme in a league of its own!

Full disclosure: Tanya, The Mango Lady is a self-diagnosed mango-loving addict, who needs no cure.

Not all mangoes are the same though. It's one of the few fruits that appear in a myriad of shapes, sizes, and colors. There are believed to be over one thousand mango varieties around the world.

Mangoes first originated in Southern India, where the fruit is referenced in Hindu writings as far back as 4000 BC. Centuries later, the mango is still considered a sacred fruit among many cultures in southern Asia.

In the United States, mangoes have been grown for a little more than a century, and mainly flourish on a commercial scale in areas such as Florida, California, Hawaii, and Puerto Rico.

The mango is such a beautiful and complex fruit that has its own unwritten language. Those who appreciate a good mango know the language of mangoes. For instance, if you give an East Indian or Julie mango to a friend, that means "I care about you." If you give someone ten Hadens or twenty hairy/stringy mangoes it means "I was just in the neighborhood and brought these over as a courtesy." Learning the flavors, texture, and pleasure derived from each mango type is like studying a gemstone collection to identify your prized possession among many stones! Decoding the language of mangoes makes the mango experience even richer and deeper when you encounter this fleshly jewel.

Let's make this clear, I'm not some mango crazed fanatic. The nutritional benefits of mangoes speak to the superiority of this impressive fruit. It needs no defense or public opinion poll. Mangoes are a super fruit and an excellent source of Vitamins A and C, a good source of fiber and contains Vitamin B-6 (11% of the daily recommended intake) which promotes the production of serotonin. This hormone elevates your mood, so mangoes are not just delicious, but also a great way to improve your overall well-being.

The fruit is also a great source of beta-carotene and contains powerful antioxidants that have the capability of neutralizing free radicals and prevents premature aging. That's right! Mangoes have anti-aging properties, so get your mango-licious consumption on. Who would not love a fruit packed with goodness that brings out your beauty and makes you feel fabulous?

So, you're probably sitting there thinking "goodness gracious, this lady has got to be the biggest mango lover this side of the Milky Way." My friend, I can't disagree. I have had a love affair with mangoes all my life. However, I assure you, I am NOT alone! The baseball, football, and basketball league fan base collectively, has nothing on the mango mania fan base across the globe.

With all the aforementioned splendor, the mango also serves as a fantastic metaphor for the seasons of life we each will encounter at some point. Just like life, the mango takes on many stages of development. Just think about this: there are the sweet and sour stages of a mango's development--just like life. The mango grows and blossoms, sprouting green buds, then reaches sun-ripened maturity and finally meets its inevitable end--just how we grow in life.

Each mango season also provides a symbolic reminder that nature and the things we cherish experience disruption, uncertainty, and change.

However, all-natural systems have a cycle with a beginning and a definite end. There are stages of growth from planting to harvesting. In every moment of our lives, God has his timing and stages for everything under the sun. Although it may seem impossible, seasons of adversity have a beginning and an end. We go through stages of change with each adversity. Often, we emerge from each ordeal far different than we began. Even in seasons of adversity, we can bear fruit and witness transformation of character and thinking.

Many years ago, I questioned why I was experiencing affliction while other people seemed to be cruising through their lives, enjoying pastures green and quiet waters with seemingly little or no adversity. Many of my friends were living it up in the clubs. They were partying and indulging in all manners of frivolity. In contrast, I spent much of my early twenties attending college and being a carefree church-hopping Christian girl. I never cursed, paid my tithe regularly, attended church faithfully, never smoked, never clubbed, and never drank. I even remained a virgin until I was married. My friends often mused I could have started an organized church called "Though shall not, and the law abiders church." Truthfully, I don't regret the path I chose and feel content my Christian lifestyle preserved me from a lot of mishaps. I found my enjoyment in being involved in church ministry, volunteering, traveling, swimming, camping, and passing time with family and friends.

However, as I entered my thirties, a sequence of life-threatening challenges I faced left me wondering: where is God? I remember feeling defiant like Job. I asked God: why me, why now and why this?

I was so focused on satisfying the letter of the law that I gave little thought to my justification for keeping God's Law. As I matured in my faith, I grew to understand the premise and motivation for pursuing a Christian lifestyle is not merely about living right, satisfying a list of *nevers* or *shall not.* I imagined going to Heaven to escape the brimstone and fire of Hell. If you're truly honest, you will admit that you have been that Christian who obeyed through fear of Hell more so than the desire to truly please God.

Through my years of affliction, I came to the conviction that if God spared my life, my motivation to follow Him would be anchored in one basic premise, my love for God and a desire to please Him. We're admonished in John 14:15, *"If you love Me, you will keep My commandments."*

Shockingly as I look back on those years, I remember feeling untouchable by Satan and his army. In my naivete, I quoted texts like Psalm 91, "*Whoever dwells in the shelter of the Most High will rest in the shadow of the Almighty*," thinking the very words would guarantee my safety and entitle me immunity and protection from any evil, illness or harm. In time I discovered that all my "never do this or that" religious proclivities were works of the flesh that did not guarantee my salvation or exempt me from adversity. In fact, Jesus promised we would encounter adversity in this life as John 16:33 declares, "*I have told you these things, so that in me you may have peace. In this world, you will have trouble. But take heart! I have overcome the world*." I believe that the peace referenced is the individual accepting the reality that adversity is part of the Christian journey. It's resting on the idea that the same Jesus who overcame this life's adversities, will give us strength and tenacity to also survive and thrive beyond our tests and trials.

God allowed me to go through seasons of adversity so I would wake from the Kool-aid drunken state and understand the heights and depth of His relentless love for sinners like me and you. God desires our surrendered will. He wants us to truly believe His desire is to prosper us and not harm us, to give us a future and a hope. Within those rough seasons when the pain, uncertainty, and disappointment was so deep, I learned to look up, truly be still, and fully listen to the word of God speak life into the dark and empty caverns of my heart.

Over a decade God guided me through successive seasons of affliction that truly taught me what it meant to fully rely on Him and not on my strength. We are often reminded in Ephesians 2:8-9 that we are saved by grace--it's a gift from God lest any of us would boast.

One of the many enlightening things I observed in each affliction is that, like mango seasons, there is room for fruit-bearing even within the bitter seasons of life. We can't always see the growth taking place when everything seems difficult and pressurized. Just as how pressure creates diamonds, the challenges we face within each season can produce new talents, maturity of character, purifying of thoughts, or manifest new ministries as a result of enlightenment we experience within that challenging season.

Whatever season of adversity you've come through, are going through right now, or will go through in the future, you must recognize that it's just that: a season. Your time of trials will not last forever. There is life, love, and abundant joy beyond our seasons of adversity.

We live in such a rushed society with stunted faith that is much like fast food or microwaved meals that we believe in things and people that offer us instant gratification. Often, we miss the blessing of growing our faith in the season because we gobble down the experience so quickly and pray impatiently for the Red Sea barrier within the season of adversity to rapidly pass. However, God is often requiring a slow sipping of our encounter and timely reflection to take the entire experience in. After all, He is performing a miracle in the parting of those floodwaters. So, sip your tea slowly, take note of the fruitful lessons, miracles and growth revealed within your season of affliction. These lessons are often powerful tools for your journey ahead that can ignite a renewed love affair with God.

Sips & Tips - Reflection Section -

In the section below, let's sip slowly and jot down your thoughts about what you've read:

- ☐ What season of adversity have you or your family personally encountered?

- ☐ What tips have you learned from that season?

Chapter Two

Preparation for Mango-licious Living: Slice from The Early Years

"I have decided to stick with love. Hate is too great a burden to bear." - Martin Luther King, Jr.

Growing up in Kingston, Jamaica, in the early 1970s and 1980s, was a true urban-island life experience. Kingston, the nation's capital, is a port city situated on the southeastern side of the island and spans over 185 square miles. With a population of over 1.2 million residents, this bustling metropolis is a far cry from the reserved rural settlements with rolling green hills and riverbanks found throughout the island.

Between the lull of reggae and dancehall beats, you could always hear the symphonic noise of higglers in the marketplace and ice cream vendors that we called fudgey-man shouting prices and haggling pedestrians to purchase their "foreign goods," which we later discovered were made locally in Jamaica. Ironically too, what starts as praises and adoring invitations to check out the street vendor's merchandise, often ended in scowls and insults if you walked away empty-handed without purchasing any items.

Mixed into the vibrant chaos of Kingston life, where goats and people often share the same pedestrian spaces, are the infamous heavily tinted taxis and buses weaving and bustling through the streets like scenes from *The Fast and The Furious*.

I grew up during the era of publicly owned Jamaica Omnibus Service (JOS). I witnessed these rectangular-shaped minibuses, slugging through the urban streets in reverent order. Those JOS buses would eventually retire. That mode of transport would later evolve into the current dancehall swagging Encava buses, with charismatic conductors hanging off the doorsteps in a synchronized balance of one hand on the door jam, a foot on the step, and a leg hanging out midway on display. It was clear the conductor's perch in the doorway was for collecting bus fares and to strategically whistle at girls passing by.

Life in Kingston was a euphoric cocktail, mixed with its share of danger, excitement, and discovery. Kingstonians understand our survival is dependent on maintaining and respecting the equilibrium of each unique part within the city's colorful tapestry. I think I learned all my urban common sense, street smart and ability to survive from growing up in Kingston. I am thankful the environment taught me how to think quickly in difficult situations, use my resources and adapt to seasons of change.

Amidst the network of congested streets, densely built commercial districts, and closely knit residential neighborhoods, we could always spot one distinct urban infrastructure: those green clusters of mango trees.

While some countries erect statues as a statement of national pride, it seems Jamaicans erect a mango tree as a conviction of *being* alive. Discussions about politics, sports, the weather, and even relationships would instinctively slip into observations or confessions about mango escapades or backyard mango raids. Seems like the mango tree is a staple on every street corner and the pride of every homeowner and renter. It's a popular Jamaican saying that if the tree does not bear fruit it should be chopped down since it serves no real purpose beyond fruit-bearing.

The most adored mango varieties such as East Indian, Julie, Blackie, and Number Eleven, were usually swiped during backyard mango raids. During our early teenage wonder years, my sister Sonji and I learned a valuable lesson in mango diplomacy. One afternoon we plotted to raid our neighbor's Julie mango tree. The house was two doors down and we were ready! Just imagine two polished young ladies who attended an all-girls high school in Kingston climbing or stoning mango trees in their neatly starched school uniforms with matching shirts and pleated skirts. But there we were: waiting for dusk. We jumped one fence and then the next until we landed in our neighbor's backyard. The tree was densely covered with mangoes so we figured no one would notice that we took two nice plump succulent mangoes near the base. We were so wide-eyed and fixated with these Julie mangoes, we didn't notice we had an audience watching the entire heist go down! The owner was peering through a window and heard the commotion under the tree as we giggled, touched, and squeezed his mangoes. Without introduction, we heard a deep voice in the dark shout "Teef!! You girls are welcome to have mangoes when you show common courtesy and politely knock on the front door. Y'all too cute to ask?"

We were so startled and embarrassed, we dropped the loot, scampered away, and took off running back home. This time, we were scaling over the fences like high jumpers in pleated skirts at the Olympics. That was the end of our mango backyard raids. We learned it was better to swallow our pride and ask than to take people's prized mangoes.

Not until I left the urban setting and visited my paternal grandmother in Saint Elizabeth, did I have my first encounter with a Robin mango. The flavor and aroma of the Robin mango has always been unparalleled. It's like an unsuspecting mixture of honey, citrus, and a hint of persimmon. Surprisingly, it grows only in the western parts of Jamaica in areas such as Saint Elizabeth, Manchester, and Westmorland. The soil composition in Kingston is so different from the bauxite-rich soil in areas like Saint Elizabeth. I have looked high and low and am, now convinced the Robin mango simply will not and cannot grow in Kingston. I loved it like a romantic summer friend and savored the taste until I could return to Saint Elizabeth on summer breaks and enjoy Robin mangoes again.

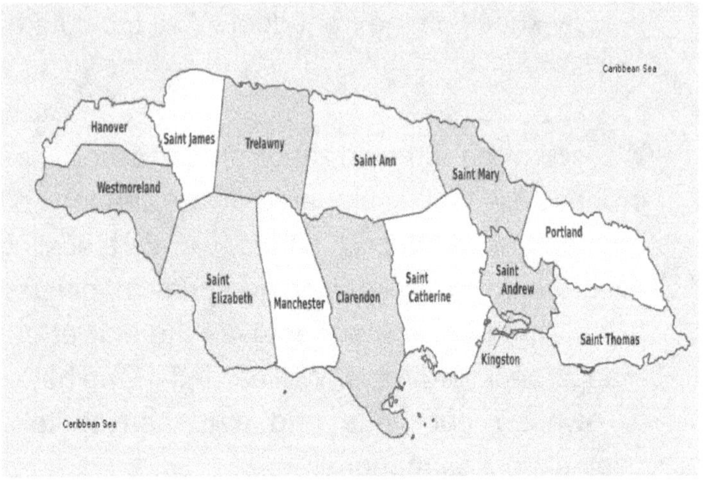

My paternal grandmother, Iney Keane Wilson, was also a mango lover. She would purchase buckets full of ripe Robin Mangoes from the vendor selling mangoes on her donkey. As kids, we would dance and lose our euphoric minds each time we would visit Grandma Iney's farm. These were treasured memories of happy carefree times.

The visits to Grandma Iney's farm all came to an end after my parents separated. Many things changed. It's interesting how as a child one of the things I mourned after my parent's bitter divorce was our infrequent visit to my grandmother's farm. I missed having access to my beloved Robin mango. To my six-year-old mind, it signified loss and separation from something I loved.

My parents' divorce is likely my earliest recollection of adversity. I still recall returning home from school with my siblings and seeing our prized collection of fish streaming down the driveway. The broken fish tank and shards of glass spilled out into the streets and we could not understand why so many beautiful fish were gasping for air as they floated down the driveway. Something so beautiful should not have been so messed up, abandoned, and discarded. This broken fish tank would symbolize our fractured minds and spirits as we witnessed a bitter divorce.

My parents endured many unstable years of marriage. My parents' relationship began as a blissful courtship when they became friends at MICO Teacher's College in Kingston. But it fizzled out over twelve years because of my father's excessive drinking and extramarital affairs.

One of those relationships resulted in my older brother Andrew being born the same year as my sister Trecia. My father courted, fictitiously married, and impregnated another woman while he was still married to my mother. My siblings and I discovered Andrew existed thirty years later.

My mother, Lolethia, was a petite and attractive registered nurse with an ambitious drive for success. She had the witty ability to seek out real estate investments and this served as her side hustle for many years. But my mother's full-time career was first in nursing and later, in pharmaceutical sales. My mother was vivacious, self-confident, and very feisty. Like my father shared a love for antique furniture collecting and vintage cars. We would all visit estate sales and our parents would collect mahogany furniture, eclectic accessories, and fine furnishings. They also bought exotic fish for their aquarium and enjoyed taking road trips around the island.

My father Isaac was a tall, handsome socialite who worked as a sales supervisor for Desnoes & Geddes, the island's leading beverage distributor of brands like Red Stripe beer and popular Kola Champagne soft drinks. He would often travel all over the island to promote the brand. IW, as many of the adoring ladies and friends would fondly call daddy, was the last boy and youngest of eight siblings. From all accounts, my father was the charismatic life of the party and the favored uncle of all the cousins, nieces, and nephews. He had few enemies and was loved by most. However, my father was a lady's man. Things had reached their breaking point when my mother filed for divorce and my father moved out and went to live with his girlfriend, Carol, who also lived in Kingston.

Unfortunately, on his way out, after the divorce, my father made the awful decision to unleash his wrath on the property. He trashed the house and left the family in a traumatic broken state. To add more insult to injury, in his anger later returned to the property, broke the front door down, and removed every article of furniture out of the house.

My maternal grandmother, Ms. Agnes who was home alone, would later give an account of how she cried and pleaded with my dad not to damage the property and take our beds and furniture. My father's violent rage left us with nothing but mattresses on the floor and no front door. It would be a few days before our front door was replaced by a carpenter.

My father would eventually fall in love again and move on and start a new family with his girlfriend Carol and have two additional children, Jhenelle and Kimberly. In total, my father had six children.

Unknown to us this traumatic experience would manifest itself in deep and painful ways throughout our childhood. My sisters and I collectively struggled with temper tantrums, insecurities, sensitivities, nightmares, bedwetting, and trouble focusing in school. It's not something we talked about with our mother or others until we were adults. The ordeal left us with deep feelings of rejection, anxiety, neglect, and shame. At school, sporting events, and at church, we were the kids with no visible father or paternal support. It was a stigma we carried throughout our entire childhood. This fractured our relationship with our father. We had nothing but contempt for him for much of our childhood. This ordeal caused us to have little trust in men in general.

To say my childhood was adversity-free would be far from the truth. Yet despite my challenges, my mother and grandmother tried their best to provide sufficient nurturing, love, and attention within our home. They both worked hard to provide us with a stable upbringing. It took years of prayer, love, encouragement, counseling, and reflection to heal from the trauma of my parents' divorce. It also took many years to recover from the financial and emotional neglect of my father.

Despite the devil's attempts to cripple me, there are undeniable forces that shaped my life to create the wholesome woman I am today. The influence of both my mother and maternal grandmother significantly impacted my life. Both of these women provided a source of inspiration that fueled my sisters and I to think big and aim high.

Our maternal grandmother Agnes Clarke steeped our home daily in prayer and melodious hymn singing. She would always be found humming or singing one of her favorite ballads like *Trust and Obey* or *Higher Ground*. I did not know then, but these songs would become lodged in my subconscious. Decades later, I could hear them playing as soothing lyrics during subsequent seasons of affliction. Grandma provided daily reinforcement of proper family values. She emphasized the importance of love, loyalty, and respect for elders within our family unit.

I vividly remember Grandma Agnes would pick fruits and vegetables from her small garden in the yard and send us to drop off parcels at the homes of other seniors living in our neighborhood. Those were seed planting years for me. In my adult years, I would later become actively involved in senior ministry through my local church. One of my greatest joys has been serving the seniors at a local nursing home with our youth group each month. This is a ministry I established in 2008 and I have kept it going for the past twelve years.

My mother's strong influence also allowed us to set distinct career goals. We achieved academically and professionally through the support of an ambitious and dedicated mother. She helped us start our lives with a clear vision of becoming leaders and homeowners. There was not a day my mother failed to remind us not to expect handouts or rely on other folks to feed us or put a pillow under our heads. She was an advocate for education and hard work. My mother would develop a successful career as a pharmaceutical representative gaining many awards in sales across the Caribbean. As children, my mother would show us her paycheck and remind us the only true reward is not winning a lotto ticket. She would remind us that a paycheck was our earned reward. It is what you worked for and earned every month through honest labor. She reinforced through her professional success that laziness and acts of entitlement would only lead to poverty.

After migrating to America in 1993, my sisters Sonji, Trecia, and I all attended college. I started my first year of college at 16; Sonji, 17; and Trecia, 19. We pursued professional career paths, and all purchased our first homes before we turned 26. My sisters both pursued careers in nursing like my mother. I pursued a career in urban planning after completing a bachelor's degree in economics from Florida Atlantic

University and a master's degree in urban planning from the University of Maryland. I've spent the last twenty years in the public sector pouring into developing cities and towns throughout the United States I have even had the opportunity to work internationally in China. Becoming an urban planner is a decision I have never regretted. One of my greatest joys is impacting communities through fair and equitable policies, programs, and projects that enhance the quality of life for residents and businesses. My success is a testament to my mother's insistence that we put our trust in God, invest in a good education, work hard and make solid real estate investments. Her motivation and tenacity paved the way for us to build stable foundations, equity and secure our share of the American Dream.

The collective efforts of my mother and grandmother played a significant role in our personal development, spiritual foundation, and aspirational life goals. We undoubtedly owe them a debt of gratitude for all they taught us in setting a clear vision, persevering with grit, and being determined to reach our life goals despite disruption or set back. These are all traits and philosophies we pass on to our children.

Unfortunately, even after all that has transpired my father has never apologized for his reckless rage, vandalism, and destructive acts of violence. Nor has he acknowledged how much that incident and the subsequent years of abandonment and neglect emotionally injured our family. We grew distant from our father for many years because dealing with him and his denial was a painful reminder of the past. It would take many years to heal the hurt and mend the fracture left by that painful ordeal.

I am thankful that within the last decade, with the birth of my children, there has been noted progress and effort made to forge a relationship with my father. I purposed in my heart not to be held captive by the consuming spirit of hatred and hurt or pass those feelings on to my children. I see in many ways how my father minimized what happened in the past to pacify the damage he caused to our family unit. I think in my father's senior years, the time has allowed him to reflect on the past. It has allowed him to consider the damage and hurt he caused. Despite the pain inflicted on our family, I truly believe my father has a good heart. I am happy to know he recently got baptized and gave his life to the Lord. My father, like many, is a good man who made reckless choices with long-lasting indelible consequences.

Despite that turbulent season of my early life, God has given me the strength and compassion to forgive my father. Today I appreciate the good I now see in him and love him beyond his broken flaws. God alone can do a new thing and mend these mangled broken family relationships. He alone can heal the justified hurt and bring life to a dead parent-child relationship. After all, in Isaiah 43:19-20 the prophet Isaiah declares “Behold, I will do a new thing; now it shall spring forth; shall ye not know it? I will even make a way in the wilderness, and rivers in the desert.”

My former pastor Henoc Paulicin once told me that harboring contempt and anger for folks who have wronged us is like drinking poison and waiting to see the other person die. I have seen so many young people stagger through life with broken hearts, fractured dreams, and displaced anger because of the hatred they carry for their fathers/mothers. It is a crippling demonic force. I refuse to let the bitterness, past disappointments, and anger of others cripple my future happiness. The greatest gift we can give ourselves and others is the gift of forgiveness.

Many years ago, I read a book called *The Hiding Place* by Holocaust survivor Corrie Ten Boom. Corrie shared her account of surviving a concentration camp in Nazi Germany. She vividly shared what it felt like to be stripped of her clothes and examined by prison guards. She watched in horror as family members were taken away to gas chambers--never to return. On one account she shared how she and her sister were sent to a flea-infested barrack. The disgusting, horrid conditions caused them to scratch themselves frantically until their skin and scalp oozed with blood. They cried and prayed for God to remove them from that unbearable, flea-infested ward. Yet as difficult as that flea-infested season was, Corrie and her sister later discovered it spared their life from the gas chambers. The evil warden avoided that wing because of the excessive infestation.

Corrie later praised the Lord for her fleas and lice-infested ward because it saved her life and prevented her from going to the gas chamber. After Corrie's miraculous survival she committed her life to spread love and forgiveness even to those German Nazis who mistreated and killed her family. Corrie shared a quote that resonated with me where she acknowledged "Deeper than the deepest pit Satan will throw us into, there is no pit so deep that God's love is not deeper still."

I cannot begin to imagine what that season of affliction must have felt like. Yet I share Corrie's belief that hatred is too great a burden to carry for others. Only the love of God can take that pain and give you peace. You have to be willing to let that pain go. A golden lesson out of my season of early childhood adversity is the importance of forgiving and asking God to pour His matchless love into my heart. God alone can heal the hurt and anger we may feel toward our offenders.

As difficult as those early years were, I now see that none of those seasons were wasted. My collective experiences: the city I grew up in, my early influences, my family dynamics, all played a significant part in preparing me to become the goal setting, determined, caring, appreciative person I am today. Those early years prepared me to overcome and persevere through subsequent seasons of adversity. I appreciate the golden seasons of sweetness that are also part of this mango-licious life. God will use all things together for our good. Even our scars, jagged edges, and broken inward parts are useful to God. Nothing is wasted from our bitter-sweet life. I'm reminded of the verse in Romans 8:28 that reminds us that God causes all things to work together for good to those who love Him and are called for His purpose.

Sips & Tips - Reflection Section -

In the section below, let's sip slowly and jot down your thoughts about what you've read:

- ☐ What season of adversity did you face in your early years?

- ☐ Who do you need to forgive from that season in your life?

Chapter Three

Once Upon a Time: Succulent Stories of Perseverance

"We are the answered prayers of our ancestors. The manifested hope and dream of our forefathers and mothers."
- Tanya the Mango Lady Blog

Throughout my childhood and beyond I have always enjoyed telling stories. My appetite for storytelling began when I was a child. I witnessed great storytellers such as writers Louise Bennet and Charles Hyatt tell dynamic Anansi Stories with such imagery and passion it would instinctively engage their audience.

Anansi is a West African folktale character. Though a trickster in every sense, Anansi was considered to be the king of telling stories. Depicted as a spider, Anansi is also one of the most important characters of West African, African American, and Caribbean folklore. What always fascinated me is the resilience and timelessness of Anansi stories. Although originating in West Africa, these stories were brought to the Caribbean by way of the Transatlantic Slave Trade. Anansi is well known for his ability to outsmart and triumph over his adversaries through his ingenuity, creativity, and wit. This culturally rich folklore, hand-me-down tales, reminds us of the grit and determination of our ancestors who despite injustice, deceit and displacement managed to persevere and progress beyond all odds.

I discovered early in life how storytelling through lighthearted humor or from a place of pain can be a cathartic release. The stories can become a testament to overcoming adversity and a gift to the listener as well. Through storytelling, we recognize the struggles of our ancestors and learn from their resilience. Their ability to overcome shaped our DNA to handle adversity and influence our ability to push past pain and seek a deeper more fulfilling life.

I recall a particular story of my family's roots and how our initial entry to North America would years later pave the way for generations to follow. Marcus Garvey said it best, “a people without a knowledge of their past is like a tree without roots.” Those ancient roots, planted firmly before I was a spec in my mother’s eye, sprang from the shores of Jamaica to the sugarcane fields of Central Florida and are now firmly planted in Miami.

As I flip through the pages of my mind, I recognize my life journey is more than simple serendipity. It was the offspring of a well-orchestrated, series of life events falling in place according to God’s ultimate plan. Like predestined seeds planted in times past, my family’s immigrant story bears fruit today from the amazing sacrifice and perseverance of generations past.

According to our family’s historian, Uncle Hugh, my family’s first entry to America dates back to my grandfather, Papa David, in the 1940s.

During World War II, many Americans were drafted into the military to fight overseas. Historians suggest over 20 percent of the pre-war workforce were now in the military, which left a significant shortage in the agricultural industry and national food supply. In the course of the war, it is reported that approximately 15 million men and women were called into the military. As a result, President Franklin D. Roosevelt declared a state of national emergency as there was a severe farm labor shortage. Desperately looking to fulfill its migratory labor shortage, the United States Department of Agriculture would eventually solicit the help of other countries and authorize the temporary importation of 75,000 Bahamians and Jamaicans to work in the Florida fields.

Meanwhile, back in Jamaica, my grandfather saw an advertisement inviting Jamaican farmers to be part of a farm worker's program in the United States. My grandfather owned more than forty acres of farmland in Manchester, Jamaica. As a small business owner, my grandfather saw this as a golden opportunity. He and many other seasoned farmers were lured in by the prospect of earning quick United States dollars which they planned to take back to Jamaica to further invest in and expand their businesses.

And so, in the early 1940s, Papa David left his wife and two children in Jamaica, boarded a ship, and headed to Florida. He later recounted to his family the fright he experienced traveling. The trip was very long, the quarters cramped, the ocean waves were rough, and the temperature was hot and clammy. Since America was at war, the route was plagued with great danger. Hearing the description of my grandfather's journey triggered a thought: how ironic it was that my grandfather would travel across the same Atlantic Ocean, by boat, like many of our enslaved ancestors' centuries before. This time the journey was not as a slave, not in physical chains, not against his will, but as a free man, making a choice and seeking an opportunity.

Florida was viewed as an important first line of defense for the southern United States, the Caribbean, and the Panama Canal. Sadly, German boats sank over twenty-four ships off of Florida's Atlantic and Gulf Coasts during that period. Historians report that many ships could be seen burning from areas along the coast.

My grandfather would later recount how frightened the passengers on board the ship were as a United States' fighter plane hovered over their vessel from the time it left Jamaica to when it arrived in Florida. This was the United States way of ensuring safe passage for the crew and passengers.

My grandfather arrived in the United States unharmed and was given a new identity. He was now a migratory laborer of the United States government, assigned a dog tag ID with a tracking number, and would work under a government contract. During the chilly winter season, my grandfather would work long shifts. He faced racial discrimination, no labor rights, and less than favorable accommodations. He was also isolated from his family and friends. Above all, my grandfather said he was homesick.

Six months later, my grandfather returned to Jamaica. With all he had experienced in the United States, he was enlightened. However, my grandfather was more than grateful for the United States funds he raised and was able to expand his business with more crops and equipment. He was even more grateful for the joy and basic freedoms he enjoyed back home in Jamaica. He did not renew his government migrant labor contract or ever return to the United States again.

It's hard to imagine what thoughts must have gone through his mind as he worked tirelessly in the sugarcane fields of Florida. He harvested and then prepared the fruits and vegetables for the market. He, like many of us, could not fully comprehend what God had in store for his children and grandchildren. I am reminded of a text in 1 Corinthians 2:9: "*Eye hath not seen, nor ear heard, neither have entered into the heart of man, the things which God has prepared for them that love him*." It's likely Grandpa David did not fully comprehend the significant role he played in supporting the United States domestically. After all, as the United States participated in World War II, the agricultural sector was in a state of emergency and the nation depended on immigrants like Grandpa David to stand in the gap, while ensuring the United States farmlands continued to generate sufficient food to feed the nation.

This timely reflection is noteworthy given the current national debate about immigration and the less than favorable light of immigrants. I recognize my grandfather did not bear arms but his determination and diligence to serve as a United States migratory laborer during World War II solidified his place in American history. I am eternally grateful for the sacrifice of my grandfather and so many other farmworkers who toiled and labored in the farmlands of Florida, supporting the agricultural sector and providing sustenance to so many American families.

The Bible has a great deal to say about immigrants and how we should treat foreigners in our midst. In Leviticus 19:33-34, it says "*Do not mistreat foreigners who are living in your land. Treat them as you would an Israelite, and love them as you love yourselves. Remember that you were once foreigners in the land of Egypt. I am the Lord your God*" and further, in Numbers 15:16, "*I am the Lord, and I consider all people the same, whether they are Israelites or foreigners living among you.*" As global citizens, our histories are all interconnected in some way. Maybe your family served in World War II or maybe like me, you have deep roots from someplace else. Our ancestors certainly epitomized what it means to live the mango-licious life. They possess the grit and tenacity that allowed them to ensure under difficult situations.

We represent the legacy and fulfilled the hope of those who walked before us. None of us can honestly hoard the credit for our successes today. We owe our gratitude and homage to those who have toiled, persevered, and laid the foundation for us. My grandfather was the first, but certainly not the last in our family to respond to the call, to join the American labor force in a critical service role.

In 1978, thirty-eight years after my grandfather's stint in Florida, my mother was recruited to work as an intensive care unit nurse in Miami. God later weaved together parts of my history and would later draw me into the line of immigrants with my own Miami story.

Chapter Four

Mango-licious Journey: Immigrant Roots Planted in The Magic City

"Storms make trees take deeper roots"
- Dolly Parton

Papa David would make his mark in history amongst thousands of imported farmworkers who toiled in fields across the United States. Their presence ensured the nation was fed during the labor shortage of the 1940s. My grandfather's journey also marked the beginning of my family's passage to the United States. Over 40 years later, our family left footprints yet again in Florida. This time it was in Miami during the 1970s.

A lot was happening in the 1970s. The year 1978, in particular, was memorable. It was the year Lionel Richie's hit song rocked the airwaves:

You're once, twice

Three times a lady

And I love you

Yes, you're once, twice

Three times a lady

And I looove you!

In 1978, those tasty bite-size little White Castle sliders sold for a whopping 0.20 cents, and a McDonald's burger sold for $1.09. Jimmy Carter was elected president that year. The hit television series *All in the Family* and *M A.S.H.* were mainstays in American homes.

Amidst the hype, headlines, and happenings of that year, 1978 was also the year my mother, Lolethia, left Jamaica in pursuit of career opportunities in Miami, Florida. Like my grandfather, my mother saw an advertisement for employment opportunities in the United States. Yet, her opportunity was different: this was an invitation for Jamaican nurses to work in Florida and further their nursing studies. In the 1970s there was an acute nursing shortage in the United States. As a result, many hospitals and private agencies resorted to importing nurses, doctors, and specialists from countries like Jamaica, Bangladesh, and the Philippines to fill the labor shortfall.

My mom, who was only in her early twenties, married and a mother of three young children, felt very apprehensive about leaving Jamaica to pursue this career opportunity. Jamaica having gained independence from Britain just fifteen years prior was going through major political turmoil during the 1970s, with threats of communist socialism invading the country, severe food shortages, and roadblocks with nightly military and police curfews. Naturally, my mother was worried about her family.

Nonetheless, my father convinced my mom she should apply for a nursing job in the United States. My father felt it was a golden chance of a lifetime, that could strengthen the family's base and create greater financial security. It still weighed heavy on my mother's heart to leave her three small children behind. However, my mother applied to the program and was approved for employment as a nurse at Mercy Hospital in Miami. My mother left Jamaica with slight trepidation, a prayer, and a burning hope to pursue this great nursing opportunity in Miami. She knew nurses made much higher salaries in the United States so she would have the opportunity to send money back home to Jamaica to help support her young family.

In the Fall of 1978, my mother boarded a plane and traveled from Kingston, Jamaica to Miami to join the growing pool of immigrant workers in South Florida. This marked a major shift in my family's trajectory as immigrants pursuing a slice of the American Dream. My mother's trek was vastly different from my grandfather's journey just forty years before. There were no cane field assignments or fighter planes hovering over or overcrowded vessels braving the enemy-infested waters of the Atlantic Ocean.

This was a new chapter in my mother's life. It was my mother's first-hand, real-life encounter with the value of a solid education. Because of her preparation, she was able to secure a great job in a highly sought-after technical field. There's a popular quote that defines success as "the place where preparation meets opportunity." My mother was able to seize the opportunity because she had prepared herself with a solid higher education. She recalled how her father emphatically encouraged his children to stay in school and receive a good education. He died without ever seeing the fulfillment of his dream, but we know he would have been proud of their accomplishments. My mother was armed and ready to embrace Miami. She looked forward to the stream of opportunities that would follow for her children and family in the years to come.

My mother acknowledged that something about Miami felt familiar. The vibe of the city felt like an old familiar friend. Being from the Caribbean, she said Miami bore many similarities to Jamaica: tall palm trees, tropical weather, spicy foods, fruit markets, white sandy shorelines hugged by the turquoise waters of the Atlantic Ocean. Seemed like the ideal home away from home. Little did she anticipate or fathom the huge culture shock that awaited her in this new land.

As an island girl, her first inclination was to find an apartment near Biscayne Bay, because it was close to her job. My mother met a friendly front desk clerk at an apartment complex named Keystone Manor who assisted in processing her paperwork. He showed her the unit, turned over her keys, and made her a bona fide resident of the quiet coastal city. Several days later she returned to thank the front desk office clerk for his hospitality but was given the unfortunate news that he had been fired.

The apartment complex had a practice of not leasing units to blacks. It seems the white clerk thought my mother was an attractive, professional young nurse and in his youthful glee gave her a unit at the complex. Sadly, his act of kindness cost him his job.

My mother eventually discovered she was the first and only black resident living in that apartment complex. She was also one of the few minorities living on the eastern side of that highly segregated city during the 1970s. Her white neighbors who passed her by each day were either stoic, looked the other way, or would utter racial slurs within her hearing as a form of intimidation.

My mother grew concerned about her safety. This was such a major cultural shift and a trying time for my mother as a young black professional eager to pursue her calling. Like so many people of color living in America, she felt the paradox of living between two different worlds. There was a *work Miami* where she held the fort down as a valuable member of a medical team and saved the lives of Miamians daily.

Then there was the *other Miami* where she went home to face rejection and scorn by her own neighbors. I once asked my mother how she stayed positive with the presence of intense discrimination and racial prejudice. She admitted it was disheartening at times and she often felt like quitting. However, she kept her eyes on the prize and stayed devoted to daily prayers. My mother's tenacious drive to succeed outweighed the reality of rejection and blatant prejudice. She pledged an oath as a nurse to not harm and felt compelled to share the love with the patients and families in her care.

I suppose you could say there was a third Miami as well for black Caribbean immigrants. Your accent, food choice, music, and cultural oddities earned you the label of being an "alien" by native African Americans.

Navigating new friendships and establishing a new village was difficult. It would take time to find a safe place where she didn't feel rejected, scorned, or misunderstood. In time my mother would find a group of other immigrant friends. This group shared commonalities such as being healthcare professionals and were not judgmental or hateful. Like my mother, they made Miami their new home away from home. At the end of her assignment, a few years later, my parents agreed my mother would return home to be with our family in Jamaica. Like my grandfather, my mother was enlightened and grew to appreciate Jamaica on a deeper level after living as an immigrant in America.

As I began my journey to unpack the details of my Miami story, my mom shared a postcard with me that left me stunned. It was an old postcard from 1979 featuring a photograph of the Keystone Manor Apartment. She had sent the postcard to my father as they exchanged letters over time. For forty years that card sat in a box with other long-forgotten collectibles. The particular city is what stunned me. Until last year, I never realized the apartment complex was located in Miami. My mother had lived in the same city where I have worked since 2006 overseeing land use, public policy, and development approvals. How ironic it is the same city where my mother made history as the first black nurse on the east side of town, would become the city where her daughter would make her mark as a senior-level executive managing development across the entire city? Forty years separated my mother's travel to Florida after my grandfather's stint and forty years marked my burying professional roots in Miami after my mother's first stint. The odds of that happening were more than sheer luck or serendipity. In moments like these, I am reminded of Romans 8:28, "*All things work together for good to them that love God.*" My grandfather, working hard in the hot sugarcane fields of Central Florida during difficult seasons could not have fathomed how far his labor of love would take his family.

My family's story is rich. Our story is yet another revelation that the journey of each immigrant group is very complex. Every family's journey to achieving the American Dream varies from generation to generation. Although there are disappointments, tragedies, and at times scorn, we are propelled by the desire to succeed, achieve and enjoy a better quality of life with added financial stability for our families.

Miami continues to be an evolving city with many contradictions, complexities, and paradoxes. However, Miami stands out as a vibrant cosmopolitan hub with many opportunities. With the right preparation, opportunities can ignite new beginnings. We stand on the shoulders of our ancestors and those strong foundations laid before us. I often sit and contemplate what experience will continue to challenge the next generation to follow. Only time will tell. As we reflect on the sacrificial investments of previous generations, recognize you and I are the legacy of efforts passed. Let us proudly proclaim: *I am the answered prayers, hope, and fully manifested dream of my ancestors.*

Sips & Tips - Reflection Section -

In the section below, let's sip slowly and jot down your thoughts about what you've read:

- ☐ Who has been a major influence in your life?

- ☐ What achievement have you attained despite your season of adversity?

Chapter F i v e

Stories of Perseverance: Teeny Weeny Big Ole Blessing

"She Acts Like Summer and Walks Like Rain"
- Author Unknown

My husband and I got married in 2005. Within three years we began planning for our first child. In 2008 we were ecstatic when the doctor confirmed I was pregnant and would be expecting a baby sometime in May that year. Like all first-time parents, we were excited but would never have imagined our first introduction to parenthood would have been such an unbelievable rodeo ride.

I had a fairly normal pregnancy in the first and second trimester with usual nausea, feelings of fatigue, and constant bathroom visits but was consoled by the idea that I was growing and glowing with each new day. The journey of becoming a new mom is filled with discoveries each day. However, there was also the feeling of trepidation and wonder. With all the books and online resources, there were so many risks, discoveries, and responsibilities that come with parenting. I couldn't help but wonder if I would be a good mother with instinctive nurturing and maternal skills. I wondered if their father would be the kind attentive father I dreamed he would be. Would he be committed, loving, dependable, and present? Given my past experiences with my father, I prayed my children would find strength and security in their father. These are traits I looked for in a mate and would soon know in time.

We found out we were having a girl when I was twenty weeks pregnant. We wanted a biblical name with meaning and substance. We also wanted a name that was resume-friendly and would be easy on the tongue. We combed through so many options. After searching for many weeks, we decided on the name Moriah. It's a strong biblical and a covenant-keeping name. After all, it was at Mount Moriah that

Abraham took his faith-bound journey with his long-awaited son Isaac. Abram's son Isaac was the child of his old age promised to Sarai and Abraham twenty-five years prior.

In the book of Genesis, we are told God instructed Abraham to take his son Isaac to the top of Mount Moriah to offer a burnt sacrifice to the Lord. Once they got to the top Abraham discovered the sacrifice was to be his only son, whom he had fathered at one hundred years old. Nonetheless, Abraham acted in faith to show he was willing to offer his only son to the Lord. He believed God would raise Isaac from the dead, so he lifted the knife and stood ready to plunge but God stopped Abraham from going through with the sacrifice and provided a ram instead as an offering. Later in Israel's history, King David also selected Mount Moriah as the location to build a temple for the Lord. His son Solomon later built the first temple on Mount Moriah. This temple would serve as an important place for Jewish worship for over four hundred years until its destruction. In time we discovered the importance of my daughter's name and how it has defined her covenant-keeping life.

As the weeks progressed, we began to prepare for our baby's arrival and would collect important items such as the crib and other essentials along the way. I was scheduled to attend an out-of-town professional urban planning conference sometime in February 2008. I spent my days at work wrapping up projects and preparing for my time away. I was now twenty-eight weeks pregnant with over three months remaining.

As I slept the night before my road trip, I began having severe stomach pains. It was an intense sensation I had never felt before and I reassured myself it was gas pains. My husband made me tea, but it all came up in seconds. Soon, the pain began coming in rhythmic cramps that were so intense that I jumped out of bed and stood up. It was two in the morning when my doctor ordered me to go to the emergency room as a precaution. I was not alarmed and felt a sense of calm that this would all work out fine once I got to the hospital. My husband looked worried and grew increasingly quiet. I could tell he was scared.

As soon as I stepped out of the car, I felt a gush of water, and then I felt like I was on a downward spiraling roller coaster.

Lord don't let me have this baby today. It's too early and this baby may likely die.

The attending doctor did all he could to slow down the delivery, but it was clear that Moriah was on her way. The contraction pains felt like a million period cramps or punch in the stomach by a wrecking ball. Contractions are the most intense spasm I have ever felt. There were warning signs that we were embarking on our first major season of adversity as a young family, but we were too inexperienced to recognize the storm that was brewing.

Despite all efforts to slow the labor process, Moriah was on her way.

"Stop pushing," the doctor shouted.

And at that moment, Moriah pushed her way into the world three months ahead of schedule.

The room fell silent. Moriah was unresponsive with no vitals. Suddenly the delivery room felt like pandemonium. The room was swarming with teams of medical practitioners screaming commands, fighting feverishly to ensure this little life would survive.

Moriah was only two pounds and the umbilical cord was tightly wrapped around her little neck.

She was a mess! There were holes in her heart, bleeding in her brain and her lungs were underdeveloped.

As a new mother, I was mortified looking at this small lump of life that was hardly breathing. This was my crash landing into motherhood.

Why Lord, why me, why now, and why this?

In that crazy moment, I found clarity and began to pray. My eyes were filled with tears and I whispered, “Lord, save my baby! Don't let her die!”

My mother, who was a trained neonatal ICU nurse, was there to hold us up and encourage us during that ordeal.

We were traumatized as new parents. None of the parenting books and advice had covered this anomaly. They took Baby Moriah, quickly placed her in an isolate, and whisked her out of the room. It was as though I never gave birth. One minute I was pregnant with life moving inside me and the next I had no baby to hold or nurture. I was left feeling hollow and empty. It was traumatic and frightening for a young mother and father who had not been through anything closely remote before. This was not the romanticized picture of the labor and delivery experience I pictured and replayed a thousand times in my head. This was a battlefield, and we were facing our greatest giant ever, the mortality of our firstborn.

Moriah lived but it would be a long time before we could hold her or even take her home. For the next four months, I watched this teeny-weeny lump of life fight. She battled infections, apneas, four surgeries, and had an ostomy bag hanging from her little abdomen. Baby Moriah endured all this while tucked inside a glass-cased incubator. The incubator became her first home and I felt like it was a holding cell. I wanted so badly to take her home.

If you have ever had a child in the hospital you understand the emotions of a mother or father in that season. Every morning we would get a doctor's report and it seemed like bad news got worse with each day. Her heart rate was not stable, she had jaundice, bleeding in the brain, underdeveloped lungs, holes in her heart and she was grossly underweight. Moriah's cries were so faint it sounded like a bird screeching. Nothing can rightly describe the pain of watching in agony as your child suffers. Nothing can describe the gnawing feeling that your precious baby could suddenly die.

As she slowly grew in strength, we were hopeful Moriah would continue to progress. But one morning, my mother stopped by for a routine visit and noticed Moriah's abdomen was distended and fairly large. When my mother checked the charts, she discovered the baby's abdomen had been bloated for two days. The distention was not detected by the staff. My mother quickly shifted from worried grandmother to NICU nurse and called for the doctor.

As the doctor examined Moriah, they discovered she was constipated and had developed an infection in her intestine. She was diagnosed with a condition called necrotizing endometriosis. I had never heard that term before let alone knew how to even pronounce it. Sounded Greek to me. The condition meant her intestines were infected and she was slowly rotting on the inside. This caused bloating and immense pain. Moriah couldn't describe her pain, but she was clearly in distress. At only two weeks old and still weighing a little over two pounds, Moriah was rushed into surgery. She would go through four different procedures to remove the deteriorated areas and reconnect her intestinal tissue.

God sent my mother at the right time in that season as she had just retired three months prior. Her presence that day was God supplying what we needed before we could even think to ask. I began pumping and storing my breast milk. I was determined to be ready to nourish Moriah once she was able to drink on her own. By the next month, Moriah was able to drink my breastmilk through a tube.

Those long dark months in the NICU were difficult. As parents, we clung to each other and the Lord for encouragement and strength. What I realized at that moment is that we are not immune to adversity and a season will come without warning. I tried to imagine how God watched in agony as his only son endured the incomprehensible pain of the cross. It's comforting to know He sees our struggle, knows where we are, and does care about the details of our lives.

We also relied heavily on our family who supported us with visits, gifts, and food. We also relied on friends and our church family whose prayers were encouraging. There are distinct moments within a season when God sends support in ways that are so liberating. One such support was from Pastor Paulcin. He and his wife Belinda wrapped their arms around us with such warm support. Although we had met him briefly the prior year, when he learned of our situation, he visited the hospital on several occasions. During Pastor Paulcin's visits, he prayed with us, prayed over Moriah, and encouraged our weary souls. His visits and support filled the emptiness in our hearts. Pastor Paulcin's presence reminded us that we were loved and cared for deeply. His presence also reminded us that others were thinking and praying for us.

It would be four grueling months but once Moriah stabilized and weighed at least five pounds, she was scheduled for discharge. We were beside ourselves with glee. The long season of distress was finally coming to a close. We had weathered the storm together and learned so much while praying and interceding for our child when all seemed hopeless. We recognized in that season what Abraham must have felt like on Mount Moriah when God said "Do you trust me with the life of your child? Hand the child over to me." Mount Moriah represented the place where God declared to Abraham "I will provide." Our experience with our own Moriah challenged us with thinking "Will God provide?"

One of our greatest joys was seeing Moriah discharged and finally sent home. It's hard to believe more than a decade later, Moriah has overcome all the complications associated with her birth. She was released at three months old with no apneas or need for further surgeries. At thirteen she continues to thrive. She now weighs over one hundred and twenty pounds, is a ferocious eater, an avid reader, finalist in the school spelling bee, pianist, and an absolutely delightful child. Her miraculous journey growing with grace from a teeny-weeny preemie to a princess has been one of the biggest blessings unfolding in our lives.

Moriah is yet another testament of the unmatched love of our great Creator who can make beauty out of our ashes, trade our sorrows for joy, and gives us His strength for our fears. Whatever you are going through, please hold on in faith believing God will do just what he promised.

Sips & Tips - Reflection Section -

In the section below, let's sip slowly and jot down your thoughts about what you've read:

- ☐ What have you lost or given up in your season of adversity?

- ☐ What have you learned in letting go and letting God have His way?

Chapter Six

The Roller Coaster Ride with Cancer and The Other Woman

"Breathe, Darling. This is just a chapter. It's not your whole story."
– S. C. Lourie

Our second child, Jada, was born the following year--2009. Unlike Moriah, Jada was delivered full-term weighing a whopping seven pounds. Compared to the two-pound teeny weeny preemie I delivered the year prior, this baby seemed enormous to me. This second time around I had a beautiful pain-free labor experience. God certainly answered my prayer and showed me favor. I was terrified of the possibility of experiencing the trauma of the NICU again. I miraculously had very little labor pain and Jada seemed to have bounced into the world with wisdom, pizzazz, and tenacity. She brought added joy into our growing family.

We had a perfect delivery with zero complications. The attending doctor remarked at the ease of the delivery. She mused that I should consider having more babies since my body was designed for quick and easy deliveries. I thought to myself she needed to have flipped through my charts to note this is a far cry from the roller coaster ride I had taken just a year earlier. I was content that we had seen one of the most difficult seasons through Moriah's NICU battle and could proceed with a fairly smooth complication-free path moving forward.

I've learned seasons of adversity can come in successive pairs, sometimes trios. Life just doesn't give you a pass because you've already had a twirl in the ring. In February 2010 we were preparing for Moriah's second birthday. My girls were just one and two years old. I was thirty and looking forward to raising my girls and traveling with my husband.

I got out of the shower that morning feeling pretty good about life and the journey ahead. That day was the kind of sunny Florida morning where the air felt crisp. I was ready to get to work and tackle my to-do list. As I lathered, I noticed an odd feeling in my breast. Initially, I shrugged it off. But I returned to the spot because I knew my body and it felt hard and unusual. I called my doctor and she agreed to see me the next day. I felt anxious but still hopeful it was not anything serious. After the examination, the doctor was concerned and recommended I get an ultrasound. Again, the alarms began to sound in my mind that I was about to possibly enter another season of adversity. The doctor suggested I get a biopsy because the ultrasound showed an image that looked like a mass. As a precaution, the doctor wanted to ensure it was not malignant.

The period of waiting after a biopsy feels like a hundred years. Though it was a week I became so stressed that my body broke out into hives. I began to worry about my family and how this would impact them. Within a few days, the doctor called me for the results. He sat me down and broke the news that I had Ductal carcinoma. I became numb. I was speechless when I heard these words. Like Moriah's diagnosis, a couple of years before the words sounded Greek to me. I asked him to spell out what ductal carcinoma meant and he confirmed I had breast cancer. I was bewildered, stunned, frightened. No words can describe how crushed I felt at that moment. It felt as if God had allowed Satan to deliver yet another death blow to my life. I already endured so much before. I began to sob in the room and even when my husband tried to console me I was just numb. I couldn't think, talk or walk. It was all so overwhelming. I just left one season of adversity and cha-cha-cha-ed right into the next.

How could the very thing that nourished my kids, accentuated my femininity, and was such an important part of my womanhood now be a weapon that would threaten my health and mortality? Like many women who have been diagnosed with breast cancer, I endured the fluctuations of shock, denial, fear, sadness, anger, and finally acceptance. I accepted the fact that I had a fatal disease that could kill me. I knew if I did not regain my focus, seek medical advice and take action, things could get worse.

Truthfully the diagnosis gave me a slap of reality that life owed me nothing. Even with my best efforts to eat right, exercise, and be the poster child for health, I still got cancer! I remember thinking: T, as long as you are living, there is a possibility of dying. Challenges and adversity are a guaranteed part of this life, so girl you better live!

I was scheduled for surgery for a mastectomy and reconstruction several months later. I was terrified at the thought of having my breast removed. Shaken by the idea or being disfigured at such a young age. the operation would last for over six hours. I was stunned by the thought that I would come out of surgery a different and changed woman. Like so many women, I wondered if my husband would see me in the same sexy alluring way. I wondered if he would still find me desirable. It was a very trying time for us all.

I survived the surgery but would also require chemotherapy several months later. Nothing could have prepared me for the very dark days of chemotherapy. The hospital administered the drug through an IV. It felt like fire running through my veins. I was nauseous, lost my desire for food, and became very thin and unrecognizable. I also began to lose my hair on every conceivable part of my body. Within weeks I was bald. It's ironic to imagine how cancer is a killer and chemotherapy makes you feel like you're preparing to die.

Like the mastectomy and chemotherapy, the hair loss was also painful. I felt like a large part of me was wasting away and I was slowly becoming an unrecognizable woman.

This was such a difficult heavy strain on our relationship. Going through seasons of adversity can rob you of your identity and intimacy. A season with breast cancer can shake your marriage and relationships to the very core. I began to notice my husband tuning out of the relationship shortly after my surgeries and months of chemotherapy. He spent far more time in music and church ministries outside the home. It's like subconsciously he kept himself busy so he would not have to confront the painful reality. I see now how music and keeping busy with church activities became his coping mechanism. Those increasingly became his security blankets. Within a few years, our relationship began to slowly drift apart and neither of us knew how to bring things back to normal.

To add to an already difficult period, my husband lost his job. This brought the death blow that fractured our relationship after successive seasons of adversity. In time my husband grew increasingly despondent and resentful. He was frustrated that he couldn't find a job and lashed out at me because I was the only income earner. He became verbally abusive and belittled me with callous criticisms. I hurled back with defensive insults. I became increasingly bitter and felt all I was doing to support our family went unnoticed by the man I loved.

Despite my sacrifice to keep the family afloat, I felt unsupported, neglected, and unappreciated. These were feelings I felt in my early childhood. Regardless, I focused on recovering from cancer and keeping a roof over our heads. Our needs were very different. I needed to be reassured, after all, I had been through with my pre-term labor and cancer. I needed to know that I was loved and appreciated. He needed to feel like the head of household and feel respected. Neither of our needs was being met.

It would be five years and my husband was still without a job. At that point he stopped looking and resigned himself to staying home, playing video games, and having me care for him and the entire family. Despite counseling and prayer, we had many disagreements. Our home became unstable and very toxic. He found his escape in music and friends. I mentally checked out and found my escape in work and friends. I craved love, support, and attention. My life felt empty. I became unsure of myself and started to question if the life I had was worth living. I questioned why God saved me from cancer to live in a marriage where I felt trapped, neglected, and unloved. I became rebellious and made very poor choices. It felt like a nuclear bomb had gone off inside our home and all that was left were faint memories of the years we built a home together. We lost the will to be together and became adversaries within the home. Unfortunately, we could not withstand this toxic season of adversity and our marriage eventually ended. The series of adversities left me feeling spiritually and physically drained, discouraged, and despondent. My life felt like shifting, sand beneath my feet, taking me from levels of sweet to sour to bitter. Sadly, during my season of divorce, I did not receive much Godly encouragement from the pastoral team at the church we both attended. Instead, many of the church folks hurled ridicule and insults that were painful and damaging to my already broken state. I was emotionally bankrupt. I was ready to quit the church and repel all that seemed artificial, condemning, and intrusive.

When I felt scorned, rejected, and adrift, God sent a Christian therapist just in time to offer support. Dr. Kayla became the safe harbor I needed to anchor my mind back to Christ. Dr. Kayla reminded me that I was chosen, precious, and worthy of God's love. She recast the vision of my life being reshaped by a potter for God's honor and glory. My hope was rekindled in knowing the difficult season of divorce was not my entire story. This was merely one of many chapters I would encounter in my life. This daughter of Zion reminded me that God had other plans for me beyond just one season. The prayers and deep abiding love of my Christian therapist, true friends, and family kept me when I often felt like letting go.

With time God healed my brokenness from that tumultuous relationship. Today I stand renewed, restored, and refocused. I feel a sense of peace and unspeakable joy having experienced God's grace and His relentless love through yet another difficult season. I am a living testament to the power of prayer to heal, redeem and restore. I am so happy I can join the Psalmist in Psalm 30:11 in declaring God can turn our wailing into dancing. I rejoice today that God took me from the broken place of disease, divorce, and near-death and placed my feet on higher ground.

Sips & Tips - Reflection Section -

In the section below, let's sip slowly and jot down your thoughts about what you've read:

- ☐ Have you ever felt the sting of failure and lost all hope?

- ☐ Share Tips: How did you regain your spark and find renewed hope?

Chapter Seven

Mango-licious Mindset: Finding Love in Israel

"Seasons of adversity serve as sober reminders of the fragility of life, immortality of love and the need to be grateful for the blessing of each new day."
-Tanya The Mango Lady Blog

I love to travel abroad, learn about other cultures, and of course discover new mangoes! One of the greatest experiences I have had was visiting Israel for the first time in 2019. I have been privileged to travel to many different countries in my life, but Israel was a visit I will never forget. I have always enjoyed meeting folks from many cultures. I often find myself in conversations about cultural taboos, customs, and of course, inquire about their native mangoes.

My first visit to Israel was like stepping into a natural history museum filled with precious gems, stories, and artifacts spanning thousands of years. I quickly lost count of the significant sights and places of interest within a day. There were just so many fascinating things that amazed me about the ancient landscape, people, and of course, the food in Israel.

A visit to Israel, particularly for a Christian traveler, is a deep awakening, and a spiritual encounter that brings you into fullness with the cultural prism of Yeshua. It's fascinating to visit the sites such as the Sea of Galilee, Jerusalem, and the Dead Sea. To observe objects and customs of the region that are popularized through the lens of the Bible was a great experience. I genuinely loved it all.

Before I visited Israel, I met with an Israeli friend. I wanted traveling tips and to know what sites I needed to visit. While there I met a Jewish man named Judah. I had the pleasure of running into Judah while visiting my mentor in Miami one morning. It's one of those powerful chance encounters that left an indelible mark on my heart. As we sat and chatted about life I remarked about being a cancer survivor. Judah shared that he too was a different kind of survivor. A Holocaust survivor. His Jewish family had narrowly escaped the gas chambers in Hungary eighty years ago.

Although we had just met and hailed from vastly different cultures, Judah and I quickly developed a special bond. At that moment we possessed an unexpected familiarity. We both endured tragedy, survived pain, overcame something significant, and were undeniably GRATEFUL.

Judah's account of the ordeal dates back to 1944 when he was only thirteen months old. Since he was so young, much of his recollection came from stories told by his parents and siblings. Hungary was initially an ally of Germany along with several other nations who declared war against the west during World War II. Eventually, Hungary deflected and decided to pull away from the alliance.

Adolph Hitler, leader of Nazi Germany scorned Jewish people. He eventually invaded Hungary in 1944. Hitler began a genocide against people of Jewish descent and his fascist agenda led to World War II and the deaths of at least eleven million people, including some six million Jews.

Judah's father was a wealthy businessman who owned a factory near Budapest and employed over two hundred workers. His father was a devout man who cared for his workers. One day Nazi soldiers walked in and rounded up all the workers in the courtyard. They began detaining those of Jewish descent with the plan to kill them all. The workers loved and respected Judah's father, so they hid him in a safe place to prevent his family from being captured.

The family narrowly escaped and stayed in hiding for almost a year. It was a tragic time for Jewish families. Few gentiles would risk hiding a Jewish person for fear of being killed. The stakes were even higher for Judah's family because they were traveling and moving from one home to another with an infant who would cry out or make spontaneous moves without warning. The family lived in a chronic state of anxiety, surviving off the kindness of what Judah described as "righteous gentiles" knowing they could be caught and killed at any point.

One afternoon their safe home was invaded. A group of soldiers searched through the home looking for Jews with orders to shoot and kill on sight. Judah's mother quickly fled to the yard and hid with her children behind a stack of crates. She huddled low and counted every moment as though it was her last. Her thoughts were on her small innocent children.

God don't let them find me and kill me before my children.

As she wiped both beads of sweat and streams of tears from her face, she could hear the steps of a soldier approaching.

Judah's mother slowly looked up and saw the barrel of a gun pointed towards her. She panicked and whispered a desperate prayer to God for a miracle.

The soldier stood motionless for a few minutes just staring at his mom, then staring at the kids, then back at mom. His mother said she could tell by the soldier's expressions that his mind was in turmoil as he contemplated the ending of the story playing out before him. He perhaps thought "Should this Jewish mother and her kids die today?" What would happen if anyone heard a German officer sparing these Jews? The soldier took one last stare, held the gun firmly, and without any warning, walked away. He beckoned to the group of soldiers and simply drove away. Never looking back or flinching. Judah's mom and the kids were all frozen in fear and refused to move for some time. Their lives were spared. They knew it was nothing but a miracle from God.

During the early 1940s, over 725,000 Jewish residents lived in Hungary, with most of that population settling in the capital, Budapest. It is estimated that the fastest deportations of the Holocaust took place in Hungary, where Hungarian police throughout the country worked with German authorities to send some 437,000 Hungarian Jews to death camps between 1943 to 1944.

The family has endless stories of the many miracles they encountered while hiding and living as fugitives during the Holocaust. All of their other family members died except their immediate family. Eventually due to the efforts of folks like Raul Wallenburg, Judah and his family were able to escape the atrocities in Hungary and headed to Sweden where they lived undercover as Swedish citizens. The family eventually moved to the United States where they have lived ever since. Eventually, they were able to rebuild a successful business enterprise.

Listening to Judah retell the stories of his family's horrific encounter and reflecting on my tragedies I realize there are certain main ingredients that most resilient folks share in common. I draw strength from stories of folks like Judah who I consider to have lived a mango-licious life. These are people who have gone through great adversity in their lives and still managed to bounce back and emerge as overcomers.

Sips & Tips - Reflection Section -

In the section below, let's sip slowly and jot down your thoughts about what you've read:

- What were the most memorable o r impactful places you've visited?

- What new place (s) do you dream of visiting in the future? Jot your plan down to make it happen.

Chapter Eight

Mango-licious Mindset: A Story of Resilience, MSDHS School Shooting Survivor, Samantha Grady

"Every sunset brings with it the promise of a new dawn"

-Tanya ,The Mango Lady Blog

I am always intrigued to meet young people who epitomize what it means to live the mango-licious life.

I recently had the pleasure of chatting with a 19-year-old college student named Samantha Grady. She shared with me a tragic ordeal that took place at her high school almost two years ago, on the most unexpected day, Valentine's Day, February 14, 2018.

The nation was grief-stricken as a former student opened fire with a semi-automatic rifle in Marjory Stoneman Douglas High School (MSDHS) in Parkland, Florida, killing seventeen people and injuring seventeen others.

Samantha was a junior at MSDHS at the time. She and her friend Helena Ramsay were in their Holocaust social studies class interacting like carefree teenagers when a deranged student went on a rampage firing shots throughout their campus. The gunman fired rounds throughout the school and eventually into Samantha's classroom. Several students were hit including Samantha. She narrowly escaped after being badly wounded. Unfortunately, her friend Helena was fatally shot and killed in the rampage. Samantha believes Helena's bravery and quick thinking during the tragic shooting saved her life.

As we sat and chatted that afternoon, I was in awe at how this beautiful poised young lady could have gone through such a horrific ordeal and miraculously rebounded with such tenacity, grit, and perseverance. Samantha credits her recovery and renewed strength to her faith in God and her incredible family.

Samantha admits feeling anger when she realized her friend Helena and sixteen others died. When I asked what nuggets of advice she could share with other grief-stricken people, she emphasized how important it is to acknowledge our pain and not try to dismiss the grief or pretend all is well.

Samantha recalled how earnestly she prayed and asked God to heal her broken and aching heart. Over time, Samantha remembers receiving peace and assurance from praying and meditating on God's word despite the storm by firmly declaring, "I could not have made it through without prayer and the unyielding belief that God was still in control."

She acknowledged that when the news cameras left and the lights faded, her family's love was the tangible force that kept her from falling apart.

"It's important to surround yourself with folks who truly know and love you," Samantha said.

Her parents, Jim and Sally Grady are devoted Christians who prayed and interceded for Samantha and all the hurting families involved in the MSDHS crisis.

As Samantha recovered, she found herself slowly going back to things she enjoyed such as reading, music, painting, and cooking.

"Those are things that brought me joy amidst the sorrow," Samantha said. "You never fully get over the memories. Little things can trigger a flashback. so important to find purpose despite the unrelenting pain in your life. It's knowing and reminding yourself that God has you here for a reason and what you are going through is only temporary."

With another Valentine's Day approaching and almost two years now behind her, I was curious to hear what Samantha Grady was up to these days and catch a glimpse of her vision for the next chapter ahead. Although petite in size, Samantha is a heavy-weight champion in musical talent. She plays five instruments, sings, and released her first album *How Beautiful* at age of fourteen. This gifted nightingale dropped her second album, *Heavenly Home,* just a few years later. She looks forward to producing more music that brings individuals into a deeper worship experience with the Lord.

With aspirations to become a doctor on her mind, she's currently enrolled in college as a biology major. Samantha's dream is to someday open a clinic and provide medical care to the poor. Samantha has her eyes set on attending Loma Linda for medical school.

In her spare time, Samantha loves catching up on the latest Korean flicks, enjoys leading the children's choir at church, and connecting with her network of friends. Lady Grady, as I fondly call her, blushed as she shared dreams of being married with kids one day. She also hopes to publish her biography and travel the world. Given her tenacity, support system, and relentless drive, I think the best is yet to come for Lady Grady.

I thoroughly enjoyed our chat and give thanks for this amazing young lady. She personifies what it means to live a mango-licious life--a life of resilience. Samantha's reflection is a sober reminder of the fragility of life, the immortality of love, and the need to be grateful for the blessing of each new day.

My heartfelt prayers are with those who have lost loved ones and the countless others who still struggle through unspeakable pain. May God send ministering angels with healing vessels of peace and strength to comfort your souls.

Sips & Tips - Reflection Section -

In the section below, let's sip slowly and jot down your thoughts about what you've read:

- ☐ What hobbies or activities have you used to help you cope during difficult seasons?

- ☐ What tips would you share with others experiencing the loss of friends or family?

Chapter Nine

Mango-licious Mindset: Story of Endurance, Mable Rollins

"Even to your old age and gray hairs I am he, I am he who will sustain you. I have made you and I will carry you; I will sustain you and I will rescue you."
Isaiah 46:4

One Sunday evening, I found myself deeply engrossed in a juicy conversation with eighty-one-year-old Mable Rollins. Having grown up with my grandmother, I have such an affinity for seniors. I enjoy the living history and amazing stories they share. When I think of a resilient person with a tenacious grip on faith, love, and the pursuit of happiness, Mable stands out in my mind. She is one of those folks who personify the mango-licious mindset and what it means to survive, overcome and thrive beyond adversity.

Mable married the love of her life, Levi Rollins, at the youthful and vivacious age of seventy-six. Many imagine that lovers meet in the prime of their youth and spend a lifetime growing together. However, this love story defies all norms and serves as a vivid testament that one can find love at any age. As Mable says, "He was worth the wait." The couple is a long-standing member of the Cooper City Seventh Day Adventist Church in South Florida where they initially met and work together in ministry.

Mable, a retired accountant, was born in Jamaica but spent much of her adult years in the United States. When her first marriage ended, she remained single. She found fulfillment and contentment in the company of her children, grandchildren, church activities, and hobbies. Mable confessed to me that she had accepted her fate to live her life single and very satisfied. The last thing on her mind was getting remarried at this late stage of her life. God had other plans!

Mable chuckled as she described how Levi proposed to her. Late one evening after a workday at church Levi approached Mable and struck up a conversation. Levi, who was also born in Jamaica became single when his wife of many years died. He was eyeing Mable all afternoon and finally mustered up the courage to chat with her before she left. His intent was short and direct as he posed the following question "Do you like me? I like you." Mable was shocked and taken aback by his bold but sincere question.

However, she now admits she was also amused and enthralled with his short and direct declaration of his affection for her. Mable processed his statement and broke into a giddy girlish giggle. The thought that someone was bold enough to express feelings of affection, get their swag on and pursue her at seventy-six sent her into a youthful giggle. She said the encounter was so genuine but unexpected that it made her chuckle the entire five-mile drive home. Within months the pair were married in the company of friends and family. They had a lovely ceremony in the same church where they met as friends years before. You can tell by the hand holding, eye contact, and constant smiles that the love is still very fresh and on fire.

Mable marvels over how fairytale-like her life now seems. She gives all glory and honor to God for preserving her life to be able to enjoy this season of joy and sweetness. In a very solemn and moving tone, Mable became reflective recalling the tragic and near-death experience she endured on September 1, 1957.

Mable was only 18 and an active member of the Holy Name Society of St. Anne's Roman Catholic Church in Kingston. She and many of the members were invited to participate in communion at a church in Montego Bay. As a devout Catholic, she was eager to serve and assist with the sacred ordinance of services at another congregation. However, her aunt, who served as her guardian, was reluctant to send her away. Her aunt was worried Mable's father would be upset if anything happened to her. Nonetheless, Mable assured her aunt all would be well. Her aunt allowed her to go on the trip. The group boarded the train at the Kingston Railway Station for an all-day trip to Montego Bay under the guidance of their pastor, the Reverend Father Charles Earle.

The day was joyful and sunny. After the communion, many young people decided to visit the beach before returning home to Kingston. Mable, a more reserved teen decided to skip the beach excursion and instead cleaned up at the church until it was time to leave. She recalls when they boarded the train, she noted a rowdy bunch of gangsters who were suspected to be pickpockets. She recounts how their behavior was so outrageous they wreaked havoc on the other passengers. The criminals were said to have caused such unruly disturbance during the trip that a priest declared that the wrath of God would surely descend on them. He was unaware at the time, but that statement would eventually become prophetic.

There were 1,600 passengers on the train that day--a number that far exceeded the carrying capacity. Interestingly the limit for each of the twelve cars was eighty people with a maximum carrying capacity of around 960 persons. At approximately 11:30 p.m. on the train's return home to Kingston, as the two diesel engines and twelve wooden cars neared the quiet town of Kendal, Manchester, three whistle blasts signaled the journey's abrupt and tragic end. As the train was turning a bend within minutes, it picked up speed and derailed. Many passengers were thrown from the cabins and fragments of human bodies were strewn among scores of twisted metal. Close to two hundred people lost their lives, and seven hundred sustained injuries in what was described as the worst rail disaster in Jamaica's history. And, at the time, it was the second-worst rail disaster in the world.

Mable remembers hearing the brakes screech and the passengers flying everywhere. She said a quick prayer, made the sign of the cross, and held on. There was complete and absolute chaos as the train tossed and spun out of control. When the tragedy ended, she was miraculously the only survivor left in that cabin to tell the story. Everyone else had been killed.

Mable said she looked out the train window and saw a man below who told her to stay inside until he got help. Instead of waiting, she jumped from the train window. Thankfully he was able to catch her before she hit the ground. As he placed her at the side of the road she was shaking and felt completely numb from the shock. Yet in her haze Mable noticed several criminals in the distance raiding the bodies of the dead and injured passengers, stealing their possessions. She could see the assailants heading in her direction. Fearing for her life Mable ran quickly away from the scene and fell into a hole where she stayed in hiding until it was safe to emerge. She connected with other members of her group and headed back to Kingston.

Based on the investigation report, the cause of the crash was later determined to be the accidental closure of an angled wheel (brake) cock that had been placed incorrectly. Some survivors believed the criminals who were on the train may have tampered with that angle brake while en route to Montego Bay. Although these accounts could not be confirmed, and no one was officially charged, some things were known for sure: the train was grossly overcrowded. There were approximately 130 passengers per car when there should have been only eighty.

Although sixty-three years have passed, Mable is brought to tears when she recalls that horrific accident dubbed the infamous Kendall Train Crash. What started as a beautiful church trip ended in such a tragic and traumatic event. When I asked Mable how she survived that traumatic season and is now able to enjoy this chapter of her life, she admits it was prayer, faith, and her family that brought her through. Mable acknowledges she could not have made it through without the hand of God shielding and protecting her from then until now.

I am reminded through Mable's story of the unpredictability of each season of our lives. Yet even as unpredictable as life can be, in the end, it can be so much more beautiful and rewarding than the beginning. Though our lives are often riddled with tragedy Mable's story is yet another reminder that there is still abundant sweetness remaining in this life beyond those harsh and tragic seasons we face. She is now enjoying her golden years as a newlywed with the husband of her dreams, good friends, and a wonderful family. She admonishes others to believe and hope in the promises of God and recites Psalm 16:11, "*In Him is the fullness of joy.*"

<u>Sips & Tips - Reflection Section -</u>

In the section below, let's sip slowly and jot down your thoughts about what you've read:

- ☐ What miracle are you grateful for despite your tragedy?

- ☐ How have you turned your tragedy into a ministry or an initiative to encourage others?

Chapter Ten

Mango-licious Reflections: Lessons Learned

"Think Big, but dream bigger about your future."
-Susan Gooding-Liburd, CPA

Mango season is in full swing in Miami. It's a lovely day to be sitting in the shade of my favorite mango tree, indulging in a delightful bowl of sweet Valencia Pride mangoes. I am rocking to the melodious rhythm of an old familiar tune called *Just the Way You Are* by Taurus Riley. My life feels just right.

Reminiscing on the previous seasons of my life, I count it all joy for having survived some tumultuous times. Large or small, subtle or deep, the collective sum of my life experiences has led me to a place of happiness, freedom, and hope.

There are so many lessons learned from surviving and thriving beyond my seasons of adversity.

It's still a great time to shift our paradigm, sip slowly and explore the varied possibilities of what each season brings! Below are lessons learned, tips and takeaways from surviving, and thriving beyond my seasons of adversity:

1. SET CLEAR OBJECTIVES FOR YOUR LIFE

Begin with the end.

In the book, *Seven Habits of Highly Effective People*, I love how Stephen Covey admonishes success seekers to “begin with the end in mind.” In essence, we should start with a clear destination. Covey says we can use our imagination to develop a vision of what we want to become and use our conscience to decide what values will guide us. The mango-licious mindset is to set clear goals that are not abandoned or abolished despite our seasons of adversity. We relish the sweetness in life and plan for a future that is bright, fulfilling, and prosperous.

2. GET A GRIP ON REALITY

Recognize crisis as being inevitable. It's a useless, exhausting waste of time, thought and energy to worry about things we cannot change or nurture the pain others have caused us. Your current crisis may not be a quickie. Wishing it away, denying it is happening, or blaming others will not change a thing. Seek healing in forgiveness. Prepare for the long haul. Acknowledge it is here, gather the information you need, and determine how to best manage the crisis or make your next move.

3. FIND REFUGE

Even during a crisis, we can find places of refuge. I find peace in prayer and journaling. I keep a prayer journal where I record a daily petition for myself or others. Next to the entry, I pencil in a bible promise. It is my record of God's faithfulness in my life that reminds me God is still in control of all my seasons. Psalm 46 states, "*God is our refuge and strength, A very present help in trouble. Therefore, we will not fear*" We find refuge in knowing that by God's grace, morning is sure to come.

4. RECOGNIZE THE VALUE IN EACH SEASON

Nothing should be wasted. Ever heard the adage, "A crisis is a terrible thing to waste"? Resilient folks often use crises to help them climb higher heights and achieve greatness.

Write that book, buy that house, blog about your leadership experience, start that catering business, release your inner artist!

God will not waste any part of your life. Go for it.

5. EMBRACE THE MANGO-LICIOUS LIFE

It's a fierce resolve to never give up, accept defeat or play the victim in the face of adversity. The mango-licious mindset allows us to glean value from every experience, journey through the pain, and recognize that better days are ahead. Humans are designed to bounce back. And you will. My life has been nothing but unpredictable. My expectation for the future is that the best is still yet to come. In the meanwhile, I will endeavor to sip, reflect and embrace the undiscovered sweetness left to be explored in the mango seasons ahead.

Sips & Tips - Reflection Section -

In the section below, let's sip slowly and jot down your thoughts about what you've read:

- ☐ What was your greatest takeaway from the tips shared in the lessons learned section?

- ☐ What new tips will you apply to your life moving forward?

www.ingramcontent.com/pod-product-compliance
Lightning Source LLC
LaVergne TN
LVHW010627100826
845148LV00014B/3147

* 9 7 8 1 7 3 5 7 6 1 6 2 6 *